WHAT DOESN'T KILL YOU MAKES YOU HIGH

A JOURNEY THROUGH THE MIND OF AN OVERTHINKER

MIDHUN THOTATHIL

Made with ♥ on the Notion Press Platform
www.notionpress.com

Contents

Contents

Note From The Poet

These poems are the result of overthinking and a healthy dose of emotional investment.

If you are someone who feels everything more deeply, then you are not alone.

I believe, we do more than just live, when we create or become part of art.

It is often a way of being more than we're "supposed to be."

Like the birds who can sing, and the mosses that paint landscapes simply by existing on an otherwise ordinary rock.

Or maybe it's all just in my head.

Wishing you happy reading.

1. What doesn't kill you makes you high

It's a long sprint, run as fast as you can.
You cannot stop, your breasts be damned.
Trying to catch it like a gibbon,
You will never reach the ribbon.

Or maybe, you can slow down,
Sometimes, even bow down.
Pick up a nice-looking stone,
One you cannot sell or pawn.

Lick a frog, don't be shy,
What doesn't kill you makes you high.
It doesn't make any sense,
Isn't that always the defense?

There is a rat race, they say,
And so-called woke, showing way.
But even if you win, you're the same.
Same old rat, without any shame.

2. The Red Cloth

My mother once bought me a cloth.
It was a bright red one, like the sunset.

I had other clothes too, you know.
But I loved this one the most.

I would wear it again and again and again.
So much so that it was no longer red.

One fine day I outgrew it, the cloth.
My mother was happy, I was growing.

I wanted to wear it a little longer.
And I tried, but it tore on the side.

I never wore any red again.
Infact I stopped wearing clothes.

I then ran naked through the earth.
Feeling the wind on my skin.

I didn't want to wear the skin as well.
So I shed my skin and ran again.

I felt a little pain in my flesh.
So I removed them all, on the way.

I found the organs, a little distracting.
So I fed them to the hungry crows.

I then understood my bones are heavy
So I stacked them neatly, under the tree.

I was now just a running spirit.
And the spirit reminded me, that.

My mother once bought me a cloth.
It was a bright red one, like the sunset.

3. Between My Lips

I hold the brown leaves between my lips,

The way a womanizer holds those hips.

Every smoke I take in becomes my breath,

And like a scar, it marks a stain on my teeth.

Somewhere between the fire and the ashes,

I found myself numb, like frozen eyelashes.

While I held onto this invisible grip,

Like a ringmaster of the circus without a whip,

I could feel humanity's death wish

Growing inside, like the smell of rotten fish.

I could feel it crawling beneath my skin—

The love for destruction, war, and the need behind every sin.

With this burden, I took a cigarette and lit,

To relive it all again—the fire, the smoke, and every bit.

4. It

The trees are not special, nor are the mountains.
The lakes between are not pretty, nor the silent rains.

What makes the moon poetic and romantic?
Or the wine sexy and erotic?

No act exists without a spectator.
And nothing is beautiful without a beholder.

Often, everything becomes normal and plain—
The joy, the pain, and every bloodstain.

We do not seek anything or any experience.
It's just that life itself is a boring recurrence.

We want to live many lives and appreciate it,
Because everything that is yours is never "it."

5. When the Time Comes

Maybe you won't do what creates history—
Wealth and royalty, or power and pride.
Maybe you won't make many proud—
The masses, or your long-dead forefathers.
Maybe you will have a small world
Where you know everyone's good.
Maybe this is who you are, no more no less,
For this is the story of many.
Maybe, when the time comes—and it will—
You will have a home and witnesses to your life.
And for this death, is what we live for.
And for this full life, we die for.

6. Dog and tail

This world is not cruel, just poor.
Your enemy isn't another human, but time.
Dream carefully and chase courageously.
If anything goes wrong, you'll have nothing.
If it goes right, you'll have nothing and more.

7. US

I don't believe you—not because you're lying,

I don't believe you—not because I can't handle the truth.

I don't believe you because you told me not to believe.

In this world made by gods, it's always the humans,

The humans whose names I do not know,

The humans who share no blood with me,

The humans broken beyond repair…

They all come to my rescue.

8. Broken Poetry

Every time I try to turn my

Pen into a sword,

I remember I cannot

Afford any iron!

9. All About the Night

When the moon and wolves are out,
That is when you'll begin this
Journey.
It isn't spiritual; the best I can give
You is painful.
In your bed, you lie, knowing the
Truth.
The past, the future, and the present,
Rapidly shifting emotions and
A long-haul conversation.
You are vulnerable, lovable, and
Breakable.
You are naked, aroused, and the
Night demands pleasure.
Somewhere in this journey, you'll fall
Asleep—
To wake up, dress up, and show up as
Ordinary.

10. The Pleaser

I always wonder, why is
Everything so heavy?
My shoulders, my eyes, mornings,
And nights.
Is it the grind I keep grinding,
Or the unspoken words I hold inside?
I blame it on my glorified tragedies,
Sometimes on my people-pleasing personality.
But maybe it's none of these.
Maybe I'm just a rebel trying to be a monk.
In a heaven full of sinners.

11. The line

Draw your thin lines with love.
If you feel it's not right, erase it.
Erase it with humility and dignity.
The canvas would still exist.
Despite of your mistakes.

12. The ride

This journey my friend is a tough one.
Irrational in every way you see.
It does make sense to you.
It makes sense only to you.
So the mind you have has to be strong
Like a flower inside Chernobyl.

13. The Inner War

Have you seen politics in its naked form?
The filthiest weapon, reeking of sin.
Yet it is not uncommon, like a storm—
The final resort, the sure way to win.

In the markets, you cannot hear the whispers;
You see them—hungry men screaming at each other.
In corporate halls, they pretend to be listeners,
Young boys and girls, trying to be cold as the old man.

Where does it all end, you may ask.
You shouldn't—because you've forgotten where it began.
That's the beauty of power; all you want is a grasp,
But like a moth emerging from a carcass,

You will mistake the lamp for the moon,
And lose your way in the day.

14. Laugh and Cry

It's a grand, grand scheme.

Nah, it's a puny little comedy.

Look around, there is no theme.

Just imitations and parody.

We all just see the cream.

Underneath, it's really bloody.

We do, sometimes, dream.

And wake up all moody.

Humans can whisper and scream.

And still, they are all

bloody lonely.

15. The Artist's Muse

The greatest tragedy is not death.
Or losing someone or everyone.

It's this micro brewing we do every day,
Filled with relevance and practicality.

Like smoking a cigarette.
It has nothing to do with life or love.

But you still do it for the smoke and ashes.
For the definition that changes with time.

Time is an artist, sad and immortal.
Tricks you into believing you are his muse.

You think you are the art, in his canvas,
But in the end, you're the leftover paint,

Which he washes off from his brush,
Without any regret, without a second thought.

16. Circle

Then god whispered about light.
We were left to figure out the right.
The blurred lines became sin.
It is not! just let us all win.

We made the ink the shapes,
The words and colourful drapes.
And within this lies our world—
For all of us, warm and cold.

We were great once and now just cynical.
For some it's all philosophical.
Everything is shallow and less physical.
Think we are safe inside this circle.

17. On a Serious Note

You will get that woman,
The one you need.
And you would not be ready.

Now, to not lose her is a battle.
A fight for love, a fight for time.
That is where everything will begin.
Finding your way, back to yourself.

The child in you is counting.
The task, my love, is daunting.
If you are a man, then just listen.
You can't attain peace without war.

18. Seasons

In a year or two it will happen, trust me.

A decade later, a voice said, bite me.

I can feel it all, I don't want to.

I can see them all, I can't do.

I can't learn all the tricks and hacks.

Do not interpret these are facts!

Who am I talking to all the time.

How can a chatterbox not be fine?

Maybe I am the reason for my seasons

Why else to cry on a spring, without reasons?

19. Fair Way

I don't own the sky.

Yet the clouds behave like my own.

I don't own the night.

Yet the stars look like my roof.

I don't own the Ocean.

Yet the salt melts in my tongue.

I don't own the days of the week.

Yet they pass through my soul.

I don't own the women.

Yet they make my knees weak.

I don't own anything at all.

Yet they all make me.

20. Stress and Strain

Why are the dreams so expensive?
And the currency, always pain?
Sacrifices and sleepless nights.
A never-ending path, nothing to gain.
How to truly live this life?
Is this special existence in vain.
The surprises starts hurting you.
No more fun, just stress and strain.

21. The Artist

The crimson sunset of the west hill
Red wine which will keep you still.
They pluck and fill and leave them.
But never touching their stem.
That's how the nectar is made.
With grapes and yeast in shade.
But then they add the secret ingredient.
To surrender to nature, be obedient.
A touch of excellence it is.
After years they'll create bliss.
People drink not to forget the sin.
They drink to remember they'll never win.
Their fight is not loud or bright.
It's sad and their chests are tight.
But when the last hope dies.
Humans hold to art, and they cry.

22. THE END AND BEGINNING

Once there was a star, old and wise.

His time was up, so was his space.

The little stars gathered around.

Singing the farewell song in round.

What happens when you explode?

Asked a tiny planet, yet to corrode.

After I die this space will become hotter.

And you should wait till it gets better.

And then on my dust, a world will be born.

Beings with my body, I'll never be gone.

They will write about this time, a poem.

I'll read it through their eyes, with them.

23. Writings on the abyss

Sometimes I wish, if I had a little piece of soul.

On which I could write the whole.

Love and life that never happened.

With my blood as ink and time as pen.

24. Like A Poet

The wind blows different, when you're hopeless.

Gives you chills and makes you feel spineless.

You long for touch, from the right one.

Afraid to fail, for it's a million to none.

To be alone among so many faces.

But some day you'll see, it all ceases.

You'll smile one night unapologetically.

Something most men don't do, typically.

The dry earth will blossom again.

You'll forget the Umbrella and it'll rain.

In that rain you'll dance, perform a duet.

Once again you shall romance like a poet.

25. Annoying Friend

I can perceive only the aesthetic form,
was I selfish to be mad or sad?
One fine day you chose to step it up,
to travel to the other side.
You were still around in the air,
but not too close, not tangible.
All those smiles, what did them mean?
you climbed above hopes and lies.
Now long days make me wonder,
do you still enjoy in your new form?
I'll not write letter, you don't like to read-
just questions, answer them, when we meet.

26. Be Still

When the deadly desert shows its glory,
The humped creature stands without worry.
And when the sky pours with all its pride,
The frog begins to sing, refusing to hide.
So why can't we just be?
Why does the mind go wee?
The journey within is not so colorful,
And the sights are often less than beautiful.
Maybe that's what brings us fear—
The true self, feeling more like a curse.
Go to the mountains, feel the thrill;
But take the train inside—it's painful to be still.

27. War Child

How can I look up? The stars are long gone.

Men of wrath wait to see who's won.

They call my mother a German whore—

For ages, she'll live as a dirty folklore.

I knew at that moment, it was all grey;

Like the others, she, too, was prey.

I asked her why they hate us, these people.

The answer's a story, and I can't be subtle.

About how gods disappeared while she screamed,

A nightmare so chilling, if it were filmed.

She ran and ran, searching for a place to hide,

And when it was over, she was a war child.

28. Only love

We learn to love, and we learn to hate;
Without that, we'd be a blank slate.
It's always people and their actions—
Some live in love and all its satisfactions.
My old lady once showed me an old love story,
A story that never dulled, never lost its glory.
They built their world, their own little nest,
A place to grow, let go, and rest.
I saw their story in giggles and laughs—
Sometimes sad, but filled with arts and crafts.
Only life could part them, and it did,
Yet she saw the world, memories vivid.
With all this love, what to do with it?
Spread it across the world—they need it.
For all those years, so much I owe.
He was my man, my only love.

29. Mistress and Lie

Blind and convinced, besotted heart.
Rewritten rules with sins of his past.
Nothing weighs on him at night; it should.
The lust he cannot resist—who could?
Strongest of men on their knees, weak,
For in history, she was never meek.
Love is war and a stolen crown,
So don't look at her and frown.

A face for the world, a face for her,
One's a dream, it doesn't bother.
Those moments, comes back, and I sigh
the lady I paid for a beautiful lie.

30. Azrael

Less clothed and more courteous,

A man with a twist of fate sat beside me.

He had nothing but all the nectar of God; he spoke:

"The inner man leaves, not scarred or scared; he has got company."

He's your last friend, the great polite singularity.

"Angels, earthlings, and demons, behold!

He's quiet and merciful to the bearer bearing existence for time.

He builds monuments of grief every day

For the breathing ones, without a dime.

"Ever-smiling reaper, we shall meet again; shake my hand, and I'll be fine.

One cannot hate nor love you, for you are the blessed and the cursed.

Day and night on your side—unreal!

Both black and white truth, Azrael."

31. To Touch

Hey, little birdie, would you tell me that story
Of meadows and grasslands,
The farmer who sold his land,
Of blue waters and black sands,
The giant whales and the long sails?,
About the nights you sing to.

Hey, little birdie, why are you singing
When none of your kind listens?

We are singers, not listeners,
Like you are human, and I a bird.

32. The Voice Inside

Do you see that well? Want to get lost in its depth?

See that ocean? Want to swim till your limbs give up?

Do you want to run and keep running,

Far away to that place of no return?

You like pain, but you cannot hurt.

You can, but you can also paint.

You bask in the sun, the moon,

Yet weep over earthly things.

You drink and smoke, and smoke and drink.

You laugh high, but judge sober.

You're a billion-year-old stardust.

You're not complex; you're just noisy.

You wish you could rip apart, but that's not divine.

It's just those noises that you hear all along.

Talk to them, for we have to live forever.

33. Invisible Men

You can see hundreds of men,

Living in a thousand different worlds.

Now in some world there is no rainbow.

Some world has no rain, it's just dry.

A few of them live in heaven.

And the majority of them want to get there.

Among these people, there are a special kind.

And now these are true people of Earth.

Their world is a secret, a happy secret.

They don't chase or waste anything.

Accepting the workings of time, they live on.

Creating generations of love and kindness.

They are not your heroes or influencers.

They show up when the world needs them.

They disappear often, you can't register their face.

They are very much humans, just the invisible kind.

34. Fight or Flight

Why are you flexible like rubber?
And situations stretch you further.
If you have ever been high,
You know it sucks to come back.
You don't escape to forget things.
You escape to find the "why."
And then you get lost, in your own consciousness,
Asking "where is this thing called happiness?"
You know the pain, the misery.
You seek what might set you free.
To not hurt a human till death
Is not an ideology, but a path.
A path with no compliments,
Paved by your own darkness.

35. Two Poles

We grew from caves to paving our way to space.
And we dug deeper and deeper inside.
We scattered away when we got too close.
When we understood gods are scared of us.
So we became humble, gave it all to some.
We chose to chase something we gave away.
Something which holds this world together.
A sin done in the past by our ancestors.
Like my grandad who sold his land,
Which was right next to a highway.
If it wasn't for him, the old and wise,
We would all be really wealthy.

36. Mercy

The wind blows so that time is not still,

To remind us to wait it out; it will move too.

The night exists to hide us from the honest days,

So that you can travel beyond mere truth.

Horror is the reason why we are not light-spirited,

And it is where everything good is created for all.

In the uncertain times, when there seems to be nothing at all,

Remember life is not an act of obligations, but of mercy.

37. The beginnings

Like a stone I was dropped into existence.
To be carved upon by different hands.
First men made me a weapon, for defence.
Then slowly for offence, to capture lands.
The second men lacked obedience.
They were sculptors who carved me up.
The first ones I destroyed,
for that was what they made of me.
The second ones—I made them think.

About The Author

Midhun Sukumaran is a poet whose works delve into the depths of human emotion, the chaos of thought, and the beauty of introspection. His verses resonate with readers who seek meaning in the restless rhythms of life, written during moments of emotional peaks and noisy contemplation.